SINEAD O'C

The Turbulent career of Irish Sensation; Her Extraordinary Life Story

RYAN HAWKINS

Table of contents

iNTRODUCTION

The fabric of the music industry is ever-changing, but there are select artists that leave an indelible impact on the world, both with their incredible talent and their tumultuous personal experiences. These artists are included in the list of those who have left an indelible mark. Sinead O'Connor, an Irish superstar whose career has been a rollercoaster journey filled with victories, scandals, and profound feelings, is an example of this type of performer.

Sinead O'Connor's life was destined to be anything but ordinary from the moment she was born on December 8, 1966 in Glenageary, which is located in County Dublin, Ireland. She had a tremendous passion for music and a distinctive voice from a young age, both of which would later fascinate millions of people. She discovered comfort and purpose in singing when she was a teenager, and the activity evolved into a potent release for her feelings and ideas during that time.

In the late 1980s, she had a rapid climb to prominence, which is the best way to describe it. O'Connor's first studio album, "The Lion and the Cobra," which was released in 1987, was met with widespread praise and was responsible for introducing the world to her otherworldly, exquisitely haunting vocals. Hits such as "Mandinka" and "Troy" demonstrated her skill as a singer-songwriter and established her as a formidable competitor in the music industry.

Despite this, as her star continued to rise, so did the number of controversies that surrounded her. Sinead O'Connor frequently finds herself at conflict with the music industry, the media, and even her own fans as a result of her outspoken temperament and her intense adherence to the ideals that she holds. She courageously utilized her platform to support causes near to her heart, regardless of the repercussions, and she did everything from tearing up an image of Pope John Paul II as it was being shown live on television to speaking out against societal injustices.

This harrowing trip has not been devoid of the author's own internal battles. O'Connor's struggles with mental health disorders, family difficulties, and the journey of self-discovery have all been meticulously documented. However, even at the most difficult times in her life, she continued to shine as an artist, touching audiences on a profound level with her work.

As part of this in-depth examination of Sinead O'Connor's career, we will discuss both the highlights and the low points of her path as a musician. We will discuss her rise to the top of the charts, her development as an artist, the praise she earned, and the controversy she stoked. In addition, we will delve into her fervent advocacy and discuss how she used her voice not only to entertain but also to advocate for societal shifts and improvements.

Sinead O'Connor was a multidimensional artist whose music and troubled career have left an indelible effect on the world of music and beyond. Join us as we embark on a compelling examination of the life and legacy of Sinead O'Connor, an artist whose music and turbulent career have left an indelible mark on the world of music and beyond.

Background and Early Life

On December 8, 1966, Sinead Marie Bernadette O'Connor was born in the scenic suburb of Glenageary, which is located in County Dublin, Ireland. She was the third of five children to be born to Marie O'Connor, a dressmaker, and Sean O'Connor, an engineer. She was named after the mother. Sinead had a difficult and at times traumatic upbringing as a result of the turbulent home environment in which she grew up. This difficult childhood had a big impact on her adult life as well as her artistic expression.

Sinead O'Connor found solace in music at a young age and has continued to do so throughout her life. Singing brought her comfort as a child, and she was attracted to the unfiltered feelings that music gave her the opportunity to convey. She already exhibited great vocal aptitude at the juvenile age of five, leaving everyone who heard her enthralled by the strength and depth of her voice. She was only five years old at the time.

However, her childhood was ruined when her parents' marriage ended when she was just eight years old.

This event cast a shadow over her formative years. Sinead, when she was younger, was profoundly affected by this occurrence, which led to feelings of abandonment and emotional distress on her part. She was able to find peace in music, which provided an escape for her from the turmoil that was occurring in her personal life as she dealt with these hard circumstances.

Rise to Fame

Sinead O'Connor honed her skills and became involved in the local music scene when she was a teenager, playing in a number of bands and perfecting her technique. It didn't take long for music business insiders to take notice of her remarkable skill and unusual voice, and it wasn't long after that until she landed her first record deal.

Sinead released her first studio album in 1987, titled "The Lion and the Cobra." She was only 20 years old at the time. The album garnered positive reviews from music critics and signaled her entrance into the music industry as a formidable contender to be taken into account. Her commanding vocals and distinctive sound, which included elements of rock, pop, and

Celtic influences, were on full display in the lead single from the album, titled "Mandinka."

However, it was her rendition of the song "Nothing Compares 2 U" that shot her to the top of the charts around the world. Her performance was hauntingly lovely. The song, which had been written by Prince in the first place, was a huge success and won Sinead her first nomination for a Grammy. The music video, in which she is shown performing while crying and sporting her now-iconic shaved head, has become an enduring image of her career.

Sinead O'Connor's enigmatic persona and outspoken temperament began to attract the attention of the media as she rose to prominence in the music industry. She did not censor herself when it came to expressing her opinions on a variety of topics, ranging from social injustice to religious beliefs. In 1992, she caused a stir in the media when she refused to sing the national anthem of the United States before a concert in order to voice her disapproval of the policies of that nation. Her acts drew praise as well as criticism, further reinforcing her status as a brave and divisive public figure.

In the late 1980s and early 1990s, Sinead continued to release albums that were commercially successful. Two of these albums were titled "I Do Not Want What I Haven't Got" (1990) and "Universal Mother" (1994). Her song explored personal hardships, love, loss, and spiritual topics, and it resonated with audiences because she was real and vulnerable in her performance.

Sinead O'Connor's career was sometimes overshadowed by controversy and public scrutiny, despite the unquestionable skill and critical accolades that she received throughout her career. Her public persona was frequently at variance with the established norms of the music industry, and she remained steadfastly committed to her ideals despite the fact that they were not well received by the general public.

First Musical Endeavors

Sinead O'Connor got her start in the music business when she was young and played in Dublin bands and music groups. As a child, she threw herself into the music scene, trying out different styles and getting better at singing. During this time, she fought to find her artistic identity, and she often felt like an outsider because of how she looked and talked.

In the early 1980s, she joined the band Ton Ton Macoute, which was her first big step into singing. The varied mix of punk, reggae, and rock in the band's music gave Sinead a chance to explore her many musical influences and show how versatile her voice is. Even though her time with Ton Ton Macoute wasn't very long, it was an important step in her musical career. It helped her get in front of bigger crowds and get noticed by people in the music business.

Sinead O'Connor continued to work with other artists after she left Ton Ton Macoute. She contributed her vocals to different projects while also getting better at writing songs. During this time, she started to figure out who she was as an artist and find her own style as a singer-songwriter.

Debut Album and Critical Acclaim

Sinead O'Connor's first studio record, "The Lion and the Cobra," came out in 1987, when she was 20 years old. It was put out by Ensign/Chrysalis Records. The record was co-produced by O'Connor, Kevin Moloney, and Maria McKee. It showed off her amazing vocal range and emotional depth, and both critics and fans loved it right away.

"The Lion and the Cobra" was a bold piece that mixed rock, pop, and traditional Celtic sounds. It had strong and introspective songs like "Jackie," "Jerusalem," and "Just Like U Said It Would B." The lyrics of the album were about love, loss, and finding oneself. They were based on O'Connor's own experiences and battles.

"Mandinka," the album's first hit, got a lot of attention and put Sinead O'Connor in the spotlight. It was one of the album's best songs. "Mandinka" became a hit right away because of its catchy hooks and infectious energy, as well as O'Connor's powerful vocals and captivating stage personality.

"The Lion and the Cobra" got a lot of praise from critics. Music critics liked O'Connor's strong singing and how she didn't shy away from emotional and personal topics in her songs. The album's success made her a rising star in the music industry, and she was compared to important female artists of the time like Kate Bush and Sinéad Lohan.

Sinead O'Connor's unique style and shaved head became a part of her visual identity. They challenged traditional beauty standards and showed how she didn't care about what society thought was beautiful. She didn't want to fit the typical image of a female pop star, so she let her music and skill speak for themselves.

With the release of "The Lion and the Cobra," Sinead O'Connor's career was on the rise. She went on a successful tour to promote the record, where her powerful live performances wowed the crowds. She was known as an artist who put her heart on her shirt because of how she sang and how real she was when she was on stage.

The success of her first album gave her a chance to get involved in the international music scene. As a result, she was asked to play at big festivals and events all over the world. Sinead's hauntingly beautiful voice and thought-provoking words connected with people from all walks of life, giving her a loyal following of people who liked that she wasn't afraid to be herself.

As Sinead O'Connor's fame grew, she became more determined to use her position to talk about things that were important to her. Her passion for activism and advocacy started to take center stage, and the artist used interviews and shows to speak out against social injustices, gender inequality, and the abuse of power.

Breakthrough Hits

Sinead O'Connor's star rose quickly after the success of her first record, and she continued to make her mark on the music business with a string of big hits. These songs showed not only how good she was as a singer, but also how determined she was to use her music to talk about important things.

Sinead O'Connor's version of Prince's "Nothing Compares 2 U" became one of her most famous songs when it came out in 1990. The song was first sung by Prince in 1984, but it wasn't very well known until O'Connor gave it new life. Her emotional speech and heartbreaking openness hit a chord with people all over the world.

"Nothing Compares 2 U" became a huge hit right away. It topped the charts in many countries, and it was Sinead's first and only number-one hit in the U.S. John Maybury directed the music video for the song, which showed a close-up shot of O'Connor's face as she sang the sad words. Her shaved head and tearful performance added to the raw intensity of the video, making it an iconic visual symbol of the song's emotional depth.

Sinead O'Connor became a big star after "Nothing Compares 2 U" did well, and she also got a lot of praise from critics. The song won a lot of awards and nominations, including both Record of the Year and Song of the Year Grammy nods. It is still one of the most famous songs in music history, and Sinead's name will always be linked to it.

"The Emperor's New Clothes," a song from her second studio album "I Do Not Want What I Haven't Got" (1990), was another big hit during this time. The song's lyrics and themes made people think, which once again showed how well O'Connor could talk about personal problems in a way that was both meaningful and relatable.

Another standout track from "I Do Not Want What I Haven't Got," "I Am Stretched on Your Grave," showed that O'Connor was ready to explore Irish traditional music and mix it with modern sounds. Her emotional performance of the old song showed how much she could do with music and how proud she was of her culture.

Sinead O'Connor's songs were unmatched in their ability to show raw feeling, and it was this honesty that made her songs so powerful. Many people used her music as a way to express how they felt, and as people connected with the truth and vulnerability in her lyrics, her fan base got even stronger.

Sinead O'Connor had a very successful career, but it wasn't all smooth sailing. Her willingness to speak her mind often put her at odds with the music business and the media, which led to controversies and backlash from the public. She didn't apologize, though. She stayed true to her beliefs and used her platform to support social justice issues.

Her advocacy and action became a big part of her public image, as she spoke out against things like child abuse, domestic violence, and the power of the Catholic Church in Ireland. She worked with groups that fought for human rights, LGBTQ+ rights, and getting rid of the stigma around mental health problems.

Sinead O'Connor used her music as a strong way to say what she thought about society and her own life throughout her career. Her unwavering commitment to her beliefs won her both praise and criticism in the music business, where she challenged norms and pushed boundaries.

The Voice that Resonated
Powerful Vocals and Distinctive Style

Sinead O'Connor's music was known for her strong, haunting voice and her unique style. From the moment she appeared on the music scene, her raw, soulful voice caught the attention of people all over the world. She is a truly unique and skilled artist because she can use her singing to show a wide range of feelings.

People often compared Sinead's voice to that of a Celtic siren because of how ethereal it sounded. Whether she was singing rock songs with big choruses or quiet ballads, her voice had an honesty and openness that made people feel deeply connected to her. Her vocal range let her explore both high, delicate notes and low, resonant tones. This gave her a performance that was both engaging and emotional.

Sinead O'Connor's shaved head was one of the things that made her style stand out. At a time when female artists were often expected to follow traditional standards of beauty, O'Connor accepted a bold, androgynous look. Her shaved head became a well-known sign of her defiance against social rules and refusal to be judged by how she looked. Instead, she put all of her energy into her music, which let her skill and feelings shine.

Sinead didn't follow the rules when it came to what she wore, just like she didn't follow the rules about how she looked. She often wore simple, and sometimes even manly, clothes instead of the glitzy and revealing clothes that many female musicians wear. This failure to do what was expected of her helped her become known as a strong and uncompromising artist.

Controversies and Artistic Expression

Sinead O'Connor was often at the center of a controversy during her career. Because she was outspoken and ready to talk about taboo topics in her music and in public, she often got a lot of attention and criticism. But she never changed her mind about using her art as a way to talk about social and political issues.

In 1992, a live performance on the TV show "Saturday Night Live" was one of the most famous things that ever happened. After singing "War" by Bob Marley a cappella, she held up a picture of Pope John Paul II and tore it up. This was a reference to how the

Catholic Church handles cases of child abuse. The act caused a big fuss and a reaction from the public, especially from religious and conservative groups.

The incident showed how brave O'Connor was when she dealt with tough problems and how willing she was to stand up to institutions and authority. It also showed how willing she was to put her job and name on the line for what she believed in. Even though the act was controversial, it also showed that she was an artist who would not be stopped.

Sinead O'Connor's songs often talked about things that were very close to her heart, like love, loss, family, and her battles with her mental health. She bared her soul in her songs, letting people in on her pain and letting them feel the same way. Songs like "The Last Day of Our Acquaintance" and "Black Boys on Mopeds" showed how her own life and the world around her affected her deeply.

In her later years, O'Connor's music became more spiritual, with songs about faith, forgiveness, and inner change. Some of the songs on her 1994 album "Universal Mother," like "Fire on Babylon" and "Famine," showed her spiritual journey and her worry for social problems in Ireland and the rest of the world.

Sinead O'Connor never gave up her artistic identity, even when there were problems and the public was watching. She stayed true to her goals as a musician, using her voice to bring attention to important problems and fight for causes she cared about.

Impact on Music and Culture

Sinead O'Connor had a huge effect on music and society in general. Her powerful vocals and emotionally charged performances won her a lot of loyal fans, and people still listen to her songs today. Her contributions to alternative rock, pop, and folk music will be remembered for a long time.

Her version of "Nothing Compares 2 U" became an anthem for sadness and longing, capturing the universal feeling of lost love. The song's success not only brought her a lot of praise but also showed a whole new group of people how great Prince's songs are.

Sinead O'Connor was a leader in the way music can comment on social and political problems because she was not afraid to talk about controversial topics in her art. Her actions went against the norm and inspired other artists to use their platforms to talk about important issues.

As a supporter of social justice and human rights, O'Connor's activism and willingness to speak her mind inspired a whole generation of artists to get involved in activism and use their fame for good. She showed that artists can do more than just entertain. They can also work hard to make the world a better place.

Sinead O'Connor is a culture icon in her home country of Ireland. Her music and activism did a lot to shape the country's character and bring attention to long-standing social problems. She took on the heritage of religious and social oppression without fear, giving people who felt left out or silenced a voice.

Sinead O'Connor's career was full of ups and downs, but her authenticity and artistic ethics never changed. She dealt with the ups and downs of fame with courage and strength, never hiding her views or the problems she faced in her own life. Her story as an artist shows how music can change people's lives and how one person can make a difference in the world.

Sinead O'Connor's rocky career as an Irish star showed how talented she was as an artist and how committed she was to her views. Her strong voice, unique style, and willingness to say what she felt made her an important figure in the music business and an important part of Irish culture. As long as she keeps using her voice to fight for social change, her memory as a passionate artist and activist for a better world will live on.

Charting Success and Awards
International Recognition

As Sinead O'Connor's success continued to rise, her music became known all over the world, making her a worldwide star. Her strong vocals and emotionally charged performances crossed ethnic boundaries and connected with people from all walks of life.

Sinead O'Connor's 1990 record "I Do Not Want What I Haven't Got" was a big part of why she became famous all over the world. Not only did the album sell well, but it also got good reviews, which helped her win the prestigious Grammy Award for Best Alternative Music Album. The album's top-charting hit, "Nothing Compares 2 U," helped her become even more well-known. It was one of the most popular and well-known songs of the decade.

Her next albums, like "Am I Not Your Girl?" (1992) and "Universal Mother" (1994), were also well received, which added to her image as an artist who can do a lot of different things. These albums gave her a chance to show off her range and versatility as a singer by covering classic songs from different styles and time periods and giving them her own unique style.

The success of her albums around the world led to a lot of touring on many different countries, where she mesmerized audiences with her beautiful stage presence and emotional performances. Her shows had a raw, personal feel, with O'Connor's powerful voice taking the spotlight and leaving people in awe of her vocal skills.

Grammy Awards and Other Honors

Sinead O'Connor was nominated for several Grammy Awards over the course of her work, which showed how talented she was as an artist and singer. She won the Grammy for Best Alternative Music Album for "I Do Not Want What I Haven't Got," and she was also nominated for other important awards like Best Female Pop Vocal Performance and Best Female Rock Vocal Performance.

Besides the Grammys, O'Connor won a lot of other awards and praise from different music business groups and institutions. Awards, like Ireland's Meteor Music Awards and the UK's Ivor Novello Awards, were given to her for her work in the arts and influence on pop culture. Even with all of these awards, Sinead O'Connor stayed grounded and always stressed how important it is for an artist to stay true to themselves and use music as a way to express themselves honestly. Fans and peers respected and admired her even more because she didn't conform to business standards and stuck to what she believed in no matter what.

Top Chart Performances

Sinead O'Connor did well on the charts because of the praise she got from fans and reviewers alike. Her singles were always on the charts, making her a commercial success as well as a highly acclaimed artist.

The song "Nothing Compares 2 U" was without a doubt one of her most memorable hits. The song reached the top of the charts in many countries, including the U.S., the U.K., Canada, and Australia. It became a worldwide song about sadness and loss. Its sad lyrics and O'Connor's emotional delivery hit a nerve with listeners, making it one of the most popular records of the early 1990s.

The song "Special Cases," which she made with the British electronic group Massive Attack, also did well on the charts. The song was on Massive Attack's album "100th Window," which came out in 2003. It made it into the top 20 of the UK Singles Chart, showing that she was still popular in the early 2000s.

Also, her record "I Do Not Want What I Haven't Got" did really well on the charts. It was number one in Ireland and Australia, and it was in the top ten in the UK and the US. The success of the album made her a world star and one of the most important artists of her time.

Sinead O'Connor's skill to make songs and albums that always topped the charts showed how popular she was and how long her music would be remembered. Her fearless activism and commitment to using her platform for social change, along with her talent, made her stand out as an artist who had a deep and lasting effect on music and society.

Personal Struggles
Balancing Fame and Personal Life

As Sinead O'Connor's career climbed to new heights, the pressures of fame and the music industry began to strain her personal life. Balancing celebrity expectations with her need for privacy and emotional well-being became an ongoing issue for the Irish phenomenon.

The enormous popularity of her albums, particularly "The Lion and the Cobra" and "I Do Not Want What I Don't Have," brought Sinead unprecedented amounts of attention and scrutiny into her life. It was difficult for her to retain a sense of normalcy because to the continual media attention, paparazzi intrusion, and public curiosity with her personal choices.

Sinead was candid about her mental health difficulties, stating that she had spells of sadness and anxiety that were aggravated by the pressures of celebrity. Her own emotional well-being became inextricably connected with her music and public image as an artist noted for her emotional depth and frank lyrics.

Her provocative actions and words were frequently sensationalized in the news, leading to a narrative that portrayed her as an unstable and unpredictable character. In truth, Sinead O'Connor was dealing with the difficulties of celebrity and the emotional toll it was taking on her health. She found peace in her music and advocacy, but she also required personal space and tolerance as she dealt with the stresses of public life.

Sinead regularly underlined the necessity of keeping boundaries and protecting her sense of self in interviews. She aggressively shunned normal celebrity society and made a concerted effort to remain true to her identity as an artist, activist, and mother.

The delicate balancing dance between her public persona and inner troubles was difficult, but Sinead's genuineness and refusal to adapt to expectations won her many fans. She remained devoted to her music and used it to express her deepest emotions and thoughts, allowing her to connect with her listeners on a deep level.

Mental Health Struggles

Sinead O'Connor was honest about her struggles with mental illness throughout her life. She spoke openly about her struggles with depression, bipolar disorder, and suicidal ideation, utilizing her position to de-stigmatize mental illness and push for understanding and assistance.

Her mental health issues were not isolated episodes, but rather a continuing element of her life experience. She had multiple public breakdowns and hospitalizations, which exposed her weaknesses even further. Her artistic skills and contributions were sometimes eclipsed by the media's continuous coverage of her mental health issues.

Sinead explored the influence of mental health on her life through her music and public pronouncements. She saw music as both a therapeutic outlet and a means of communicating her feelings to others. Songs from the album "Universal Mother" such as "Fire on Babylon" and "Famine" highlight her personal journey and emotional difficulties.

Sinead's personal and forceful campaign for mental health awareness and assistance. She asked society to consider mental health as seriously as physical health and to give compassionate treatment for people suffering from mental illness. Her willingness to reveal her own troubles highlighted that, regardless of fame or achievement, mental health issues can afflict anyone.

Sinead O'Connor's mental health issues intertwined with her advocacy at times. In 2017, she shared an upsetting video on social media about her mental health difficulties and feelings of isolation. The video generated discussions among her fans about the need for better mental health support systems.

Despite the ups and downs, Sinead remained dedicated to her music and cause. She continued to utilize her platform to raise mental health awareness and to encourage others to seek assistance and support when necessary. Her candor about her own experience gave numerous people facing similar challenges a ray of hope and understanding.

Turning Points and Overcoming Difficulties

Sinead O'Connor endured multiple turning points in her stormy career that altered her personal and professional life. These key events, while frequently difficult, provided possibilities for personal development, self-discovery, and reinvention.

The publication of her album "Universal Mother" in 1994 was one of the most crucial turning points in her career. With a more spiritual and reflective tone, the album marked a change from her prior work. Songs like "Red Football" and "All Babies" explored themes of maternity, spirituality, and humanity's interconnectedness.

"Universal Mother" represented a turning point in Sinead's life. She began to remove herself from the expectations of the music industry, preferring a more introspective and experimental approach to her music. This shift reflected her own journey as she went further into her faith and sought a better understanding of herself.

Another watershed moment in her career occurred in 1999, when she was ordained as a priest in the Latin Tridentine Church. Her ordination generated even more controversy, since she took the name Mother Bernadette Mary and was chastised by religious authorities as well as the public. Her ordination was a very personal decision that reflected her spiritual convictions as well as her desire to find a sense of purpose and significance outside of music.

Her spiritual journey, however, was not without difficulties. She declared her desire to leave the Catholic Church in 2007 due to the way it handled child abuse cases and other issues. Her departure exemplified her refusal to sacrifice her views for the sake of tradition or compliance.

Sinead had personal and professional struggles in the years that followed, including public disagreements with family members and chronic mental health battles. She did, however, have triumphant moments, such as her presence at the "Hope" event in 2003, where she played alongside other artists in support of Northern Ireland peace.

Sinead announced her retirement from the music industry in 2020, claiming a desire to focus on her health and family. This decision marked the beginning of a new chapter in her life, underlining the significance of putting personal well-being ahead of professional expectations.

Despite the difficulties she experienced, Sinead O'Connor's tenacity and unflinching dedication to her artistic expression and advocacy won her followers and cemented her legacy as an iconic musician. She illustrated that, even in the face of adversity, sticking to one's ideas and utilizing one's voice for positive change can be transformative not only for oneself but also for society as a whole.

Sinead O'Connor's life and career were marked by a number of watershed moments, personal hardships, and achievements. Her powerful vocals, distinct style, and daring expression propelled her to prominence in the music industry, while her campaign for social change and mental health awareness left an indelible mark on culture and society. Sinead O'Connor remained a real and unapologetic artist despite the hurdles and scandals, using her platform to speak her truth and advocate for a better world. Her legacy as an Irish celebrity lives on, motivating countless people to embrace their individuality and use their voices to effect positive change.

Activism and Advocacy
Social and Political Causes

Sinead O'Connor's action was a big part of who she was as an artist all through her career. She used her position to speak out against social wrongs, fight for human rights, and talk about important world problems. She stood out as an artist with a strong social conscience because she was willing to face issues head-on and use her voice for change.

One of the things that was most important to O'Connor was the fight against child abuse and for children's rights. She was abused when she was a child, which is why she is so passionate about this problem. She asked people to pay more attention to cases of child abuse and urged people to put the safety and well-being of children first.

O'Connor did a lot to stop child abuse, but she also spoke out about how women were treated in society and the music business. She fought against gender stereotypes and the idea that women are things, and she stressed the importance of giving women equal chances and respect in all areas.

Also, O'Connor was a strong advocate for LGBTQ+ rights. She spoke out for the rights of LGBTQ+ people through her songs and performances, which she used to celebrate love and acceptance. "Troy," one of her songs, is seen as a song for gay rights and respect.

Sinead O'Connor was also concerned about the earth and climate change as part of her activism. In 2014, she said she was going to become a Muslim and changed her name to Shuhada' Davitt. With this statement and her ongoing work for environmental causes, she showed that she was committed to using her voice for the greater good and that she thought spirituality and nature were important.

Personal and Spiritual Evolution

Sinead O'Connor changed a lot as a person and as a spiritual being over the course of her life and work. Her journey was marked by her search for who she was, what her life meant, and how to heal. Her honesty about her own struggles and spiritual quests struck a chord with many fans, who found comfort and guidance in the way she talked about them.

In the 1990s, O'Connor's interest in faith was the most important thing she did. In 2007, she put out the album "Theology," which had songs about religion, God, and the human experience. The album had two discs: "Dublin Sessions" and "London Sessions." Each explored a different part of spirituality.

Her decision to become a priest in 1999 and her later choice to become a Muslim showed how far she had come spiritually. She was able to connect with her religion and find out more about herself because of the choices she made. But her spiritual studies were not limited to the rules of traditional religion. She took a more open-minded view of spirituality, which came out in her music, activism, and personal values.

Changing her name over the course of her work showed how she changed as a person and as a spiritual being. Each name change meant a change in who she was and a new step on her path through life. Because she was open to change and growth in both her personal life and her work, she was a constantly changing artist.

Fans liked her even more because she was honest about her issues with mental health and the problems she faced in the music business. They saw in her a real and relatable person. Sinead O'Connor stayed true to her beliefs and kept using her platform for good even when she was in the middle of issues and hard times.

Retirement and Comebacks

Sinead O'Connor quit the music business in 2003, saying she wanted to focus on her personal life and health. After years of dealing with the challenges of fame, issues, and struggles with her mental health, she decided to step out of the spotlight. Many fans and music lovers were surprised by the news, since O'Connor was at the top of her game and still had a huge fan base.

Sinead O'Connor tried to find peace away from the public eye when she was retired. She turned her attention to her family and raising her children, which brought her peace. Her choice to put her health and family life ahead of her work showed that she was determined to keep a sense of balance and authenticity in the midst of fame.

But O'Connor's leaving the music business did not mean the end of her journey as an artist. She sometimes went on TV and radio shows to talk about her life, her songs, and the things that were important to her. These appearances informed people of how long she has been around and how important her music and activism have been.

Sinead O'Connor came back to the music scene in 2005 with the release of "Throw Down Your Arms," an album of reggae songs that paid tribute to her Jamaican roots. The record showed how her music was still changing and getting more daring. With "Throw Down Your Arms," she showed that she was ready to try out new musical styles and push the limits of her art.

O'Connor didn't just make a comeback in the music world. Neil Jordan directed her first movie, an Irish thriller called "The Butcher Boy," which came out in 2009. Her performance as Mrs. Nugent won her praise from critics and showed how versatile she is as an artist.

O'Connor's whole career was built around the idea of coming back and starting over. In 2014, she put out her tenth studio record, "I'm Not Bossy, I'm the Boss." The name of the album came from the "Ban Bossy" movement, which tried to get girls and women to take on leadership roles without having to deal with gendered stereotypes. The record was another step in O'Connor's artistic journey, as she kept trying out new ideas and styles.

Influence and Legacy
Impact on Music Industry and Artists

Sinead O'Connor's influence on the music industry and on other musicians has been substantial and far-reaching. She attracted fans with her raw emotion, distinctive vocals, and bold commitment to music and activism from the moment she broke onto the scene with "The Lion and the Cobra" in 1987. One of the most notable characteristics of O'Connor's influence was her willingness to confront musical traditions and industry rules. She refused to be restricted by genre or preconceptions, defying categorization. Her music merged elements of rock, folk, pop, and soul to create a distinct and recognizable sound that resisted easy categorization. Her emotionally charged performances and powerful voice distinguish her as an artist with enormous talent and depth. O'Connor's ability to portray real emotion through her songs struck a chord with audiences, building a strong and lasting bond with her followers.

O'Connor, as an artist, was unafraid to address contentious and delicate themes in her music and public pronouncements. She used her position to raise awareness about social injustices and offer a voice to the underprivileged, from her activism against child abuse and advocacy for LGBTQ+ rights to her open comments about mental health. Her bravery in confronting these issues motivated other artists to utilize their voices for good. O'Connor's impact on the music industry extended beyond her musical accomplishments; she pioneered the use of art as a forum for social and political commentary.

In addition to her advocacy, O'Connor's influence on the music industry was seen through partnerships and contributions to the work of other artists. Her duet with Peter Gabriel on "Blood of Eden" was a career highlight for both of them, showing their vocal compatibility and artistic synergy. Her reputation as an artist who valued authenticity and uniqueness has made an indelible mark on generations of musicians who have followed in her footsteps. Artists of all genres have mentioned O'Connor as an inspiration, applauding her bravery and zeal for pushing limits in the quest of artistic expression. Sinead O'Connor's impact on the music industry and other musicians endures, with her influence seen in the work of artists who draw inspiration from her bold approach to music and her unflinching commitment to utilizing her voice for positive change.

Enduring Cultural Significance

Sinead O'Connor has enduring cultural significance that stretches beyond the music industry to numerous elements of society and popular culture. Her cultural impact can be observed in the way she defied traditional standards, pushed for social justice, and openly acknowledged her personal hardships. O'Connor's vocal criticism of the Catholic Church, as well as her advocacy for the rights of abused children, brought institutional abuse and accountability to the forefront of public consciousness. Her efforts triggered discussions on the need for greater openness and justice within religious institutions, resonating with abuse survivors and motivating others to speak up against injustice. Her support for LGBTQ+ rights has also left an enduring imprint on culture. O'Connor used her platform to advocate for equality and acceptance during a time when LGBTQ+ concerns were still neglected. Her song "Troy," which was frequently perceived as a gay rights anthem, became a symbol of hope and empowerment for the LGBTQ+ community and its supporters.

Furthermore, her candor regarding her mental health difficulties served to de-stigmatize mental illness and sparked discussions on the necessity of mental health assistance and understanding. O'Connor became a beacon of hope for those facing similar issues by sharing her own experiences, reinforcing the idea that getting help and speaking out should be encouraged, not discouraged. Sinead O'Connor's cultural importance may also be seen in her influence on fashion and style. Her unique shaved head became a symbol of defiance and independence in the music industry, challenging traditional conceptions of femininity and beauty. Her decision to wear a unique style that defied gender stereotypes pushed others to embrace their own identities and reject conventional expectations.

O'Connor's music has been frequently utilized in soundtracks and key moments of storytelling in television and film. Her emotive ballads have enhanced the emotional impact of these cinematic encounters, lending themselves to situations of loss, love, and redemption. Sinead O'Connor's cultural relevance is also shown in her influence on modern artists, who continue to be inspired by her craft and activism. Musicians, activists, and creators of many disciplines continue to be inspired by her bold approach to creation and her devotion to using her platform for good.

Remembering Sinead O'Connor

Sinead O'Connor's influence on the music industry, culture, and society as a whole has left an unforgettable imprint on many people's hearts. Remembering her legacy is about more than simply her artistic accomplishments; it is also about acknowledging the courage and authenticity she brought to her personal and professional life. Sinead O'Connor will be recognized as an artist for her powerful and passionate vocals, which could send audiences to tears. Her music explored the depths of human emotion, touching on themes like as love, heartbreak, social justice, and spirituality. Her eagerness to venture into new musical territory and defy traditions revealed her dedication to artistic growth and evolution.

Aside from her music, O'Connor's fight for social justice and neglected groups will be remembered for her honesty and compassion. She was brave to use her position to raise awareness about problems that were important to her, and her activism encouraged many people to use their voices for good. Her effect on other artists, both in Ireland and around the world, attests to her talent and authenticity's ongoing significance. Many musicians, from established stars to newcomers, regard O'Connor as an inspiration and a leader in the use of music as a medium for social and political criticism.

Her effect on fashion and style is also part of her legacy. Her striking shaved head and wardrobe choices have become an image of originality and defiance, pushing people to embrace their unique identities and reject societal norms. Sinead O'Connor's path was one of perseverance and self-discovery. Her honesty and sincerity in confronting personal hardships and mental health challenges made her a relevant and empathic figure for many. Her advocacy for mental health awareness and destigmatization continues to improve the lives of individuals who suffer similar challenges.

We remember Sinead O'Connor not only for her creative talent and accomplishments, but also for her commitment to utilizing her voice for positive change. Her influence on the music industry, culture, and society at large will be felt for centuries to come. Her legacy reminds us that artists have the ability to shape conversations, challenge norms, and inspire transformational change, and that authenticity and courage can leave an indelible impression on the world.

Conclusion

Sinead O'Connor is one of the few musicians in the annals of music history who has left an impression that is as profound as it was. She surpassed the confines of conventional artistry and became an icon of bold honesty with her seductive vocals, deep emotion, and uncompromising determination to using her voice for positive change in the world. O'Connor's journey was a monument to her uncompromising drive to self-discovery and artistic development. From her ground-breaking debut album "The Lion and the Cobra" to her subsequent musical experiments and spiritual transformation, O'Connor's trip spanned a wide range of artistic territory. She was a pioneer in the music industry and an inspiration to generations of musicians and activists alike thanks to her willingness to defy conventional standards, confront personal hardships, and campaign for social justice.

Her influence on society and culture, in addition to the timelessness of her music, will ensure that her legacy lives on. Those who have had their feelings stirred by O'Connor's artistry have been left with an indelible stamp on their hearts as a result of her unapologetic embrace of her individualism and her brave investigation of spirituality, both of which resisted easy categorization. We commemorate Sinead O'Connor's legacy as a light of hope and authenticity in a society that is frequently marked by conformity and divisiveness as we remember her now as we did when she was alive. Her music, activism, and advocacy continue to reverberate with audiences all throughout the world, urging us to utilize our voices for positive change and to embrace our authentic selves without any reservations. Sinead O'Connor has maintained her status as an everlasting icon, serving as a representation of resiliency, compassion, and the transformational power of creativity. Her transformation from the lioness to the lotus serves as a potent illustration of how, despite the challenges of life, it is possible to find inner fortitude, personal development, and aesthetic fulfillment. Her legacy will continue on, permanently imprinted in the fabric of music and culture, serving as a reminder to be unashamedly true to who we are as individuals and to continually work toward creating a world that is kinder and more compassionate.

In the sphere of music, Sinead O'Connor's name shines like a guiding star, serving as a reminder that courageous honesty and the pursuit of justice and love can leave an indelible impact on the world; a legacy that will continue to inspire and enchant generations to come in the years to come.

Printed in Great Britain
by Amazon